Summary

Total federal debt can increase in two ways. First, debt increases when the government sells debt to the public to finance budget deficits and acquire the financial resources needed to meet its obligations. This increases *debt held by the public*. Second, debt increases when the federal government issues debt to certain government accounts, such as the Social Security, Medicare, and Transportation trust funds, in exchange for their reported surpluses. This increases *debt held by government accounts*. The sum of *debt held by the public* and *debt held by government accounts* is the total federal debt. Surpluses reduce debt held by the public, while deficits raise it.

On August 2, 2011, President Obama signed the Budget Control Act of 2011 (BCA; S. 365; P.L. 112-25), after an extended debt limit episode. The federal debt had reached its legal limit on May 16, 2011, prompting Treasury Secretary Timothy Geithner to declare a debt issuance suspension period, allowing certain extraordinary measures to extend Treasury's borrowing capacity. The BCA included provisions aimed at deficit reduction and allowing the debt limit to rise between $2,100 billion and $2,400 billion in three stages, the latter two subject to congressional disapproval. Once the BCA was enacted, a presidential certification triggered a $400 billion increase, raising the debt limit to $14,694 billion. That certification also triggered a second $500 billion increase on September 22, 2011, as a disapproval measure (H.J.Res. 77) only passed the House. A January 12, 2012, presidential certification will trigger a third, $1.2 trillion, increase after 15 days unless a disapproval measure, which would be subject to veto, were enacted. On January 18, 2012, the House passed such a measure (H.J.Res. 98) on a 239-176 vote.

Congress has always placed restrictions on federal debt. The form of debt restrictions, structured as amendments to the Second Liberty Bond Act of 1917, evolved into a general debt limit in 1939. Congress has voted to raise the debt limit 11 times since 2001, due to persistent deficits and additions to federal trust funds. Congress raised the limit in June 2002, and by December 2002 the U.S. Treasury asked Congress for another increase, which passed in May 2003. In June 2004, the U.S. Treasury asked for another debt limit increase and again in October 2004. A debt limit increase was enacted on November 19, 2004. In 2005, reconciliation instructions in the FY2006 budget resolution (H.Con.Res. 95) included a debt limit increase. After warnings from the U.S. Treasury, Congress passed an increase that the President signed on March 20. In 2007, Congress approved legislation (H.J.Res. 43) to raise the debt limit by $850 billion to $9,815 billion that the President signed September 29, 2007.

The recent economic slowdown led to sharply higher deficits in recent years, which led to a series of debt limit increases. The Housing and Economic Recovery Act of 2008 (H.R. 3221), signed into law (P.L. 110-289) on July 30, 2008, included a debt limit increase. The Emergency Economic Stabilization Act of 2008 (H.R. 1424), signed into law on October 3 (P.L. 110-343), raised the debt limit again. The debt limit rose a third time in less than a year to $12,104 billion with the passage of the American Recovery and Reinvestment Act of 2009 on February 13, 2009 (ARRA; H.R. 1), which was signed into law on February 17, 2009 (P.L. 111-5).

Following this measure, the debt limit was subsequently increased by $290 billion to $12,394 billion (P.L. 111-123) in a stand-alone debt limit bill on December 28, 2009, and by $1.9 trillion to $14,294 billion on February 12, 2010 (P.L. 111-139), as part of a package that also contained the Statutory Pay-As-You-Go Act of 2010.

This report will be updated as events warrant.

Contents

Figures

Tables

Appendixes

Contacts

Introduction

The statutory debt limit applies to almost all federal debt.[1] The limit applies to federal debt held by the public (that is, debt held outside the federal government itself) and to federal debt held by the government's own accounts. Federal trust funds, such as Social Security, Medicare, Transportation, and Civil Service Retirement accounts, hold most of this internally held debt.[2] The government's surpluses or deficits determine essentially all of the change in debt held by the public.[3] The government's on-budget fiscal balance, which excludes a U.S. Postal Service net surplus or deficit and a large Social Security surplus of payroll taxes net of paid benefits, does not directly affect debt held in government accounts.[4] Increases or decreases in debt held by government accounts result from net financial flows into accounts holding the debt, such as the Social Security Trust Fund. Legal requirements and government accounting practices also affect levels of debt held by government accounts.[5]

On August 2, 2011, President Obama signed into law the Budget Control Act of 2011 (BCA; S. 365), after an extended debt limit episode. The federal debt reached its statutory limit on May 16, 2011, prompting Treasury Secretary Timothy Geithner to declare a debt issuance suspension period, allowing certain extraordinary measures to extend Treasury's borrowing capacity. The BCA included provisions aimed at deficit reduction and would allow the debt limit to rise between $2,100 billion and $2,400 billion in three stages, with the latter two subject to congressional disapproval. Two of the three increases, totaling $900 billion, have occurred.

A January 12, 2012, presidential certification will trigger a third, $1.2 trillion, increase after 15 days unless a disapproval measure, which would be subject to veto, were enacted.[6] On January 18, 2012, the House passed such a measure (H.J.Res. 98) on a 239-176 vote.

The Budget Control Act of 2011

On August 2, 2011, President Obama signed into law the Budget Control Act of 2011 (P.L. 112-25), following House approval of the measure by a vote of 269-161 on August 1, 2011, and Senate approval by a vote of 74-26 on August 2, 2011.[7] This measure included numerous

---

[1] Approximately 0.5% of total debt is excluded from debt limit coverage. The Treasury defines "Total Public Debt Subject to Limit" as "the Total Public Debt Outstanding less Unamortized Discount on Treasury Bills and Zero-Coupon Treasury Bonds, old debt issued prior to 1917, and old currency called United States Notes, as well as Debt held by the Federal Financing Bank and Guaranteed Debt." For details, see http://www.treasurydirect.gov. The debt limit is codified as 31 U.S.C. §3101.

[2] Although there are hundreds of trust funds, the overwhelming majority are very small. The 12 largest trust funds hold 98.8% of the federal debt held in government accounts.

[3] Other means of financing—including cash balance changes, seigniorage, and capitalization of financing accounts used to fund federal credit programs—have relatively little effect on the changes in debt held by the public.

[4] In future years, when some trust funds are projected to pay out more than they take in, funds that the Treasury would use to redeem those intergovernmental debts must be obtained via higher taxes or lower government spending.

[5] Trust fund surpluses by law must be invested in special federal government securities.

[6] President Barack Obama, Letter from the President to the Speaker of the House of Representatives and the President of the Senate Regarding the Debt Limit, January 12, 2012, available at http://www.whitehouse.gov/the-press-office/2012/01/12/letter-president-speaker-house-representatives-and-president-senate-rega.

[7] Consideration of this measure began on July 25, 2011, following legislation introduced by House Speaker Boehner (House Substitute Amendment to S. 627) and Majority Leader Reid (S.Amdt. 581 to S. 1323). Speaker Boehner's (continued...)

---

provisions aimed at deficit reduction, and would allow a series of increases in the debt limit of up to $2,400 billion ($2.4 trillion) subject to certain conditions.[8]

This measure includes major provisions that

- impose discretionary spending caps, enforced by automatic spending reductions, referred to as a sequester;[9]

- establish a Joint Select Committee on Deficit Reduction, whose recommendations would be eligible for expedited consideration;

- require a vote on a joint resolution on a proposed constitutional amendment to mandate a balanced federal budget;[10] and

- institute a mechanism allowing for the President and Treasury Secretary to raise the debt ceiling, subject to congressional disapproval.

Debt Limit Increases Under the BCA

The legislation provides a three-step procedure by which the debt limit can be increased. First, the debt limit was raised by $400 billion, to $14,694 billion on August 2, 2011, following a certification of the President that the debt was within $100 billion of its legal limit.[11]

A second increase of $500 billion occurred on September 22, 2011, which was also triggered by the President's certification of August 2. The second increase, scheduled for 50 days after that certification, was subject to a joint resolution of disapproval. Because such a resolution could be vetoed, blocking a debt limit increase would be challenging. The Senate rejected a disapproval measure (S.J.Res. 25) on September 8, 2011, on a 45-52 vote. The House did pass a disapproval measure (H.J.Res. 77) on a 232-186 vote, although the Senate declined to act on that measure.

In late December 2011, the debt limit came within $100 billion of its statutory limit, which triggered a provision allowing the President to issue a certification that would lead to a third

---

(...continued)

proposal passed the House on July 29, 2011, by a vote of 218-210. Neither proposal passed in the Senate.

[8] For details, see CRS Report R41965, *The Budget Control Act of 2011*, by Bill Heniff Jr., Elizabeth Rybicki, and Shannon M. Mahan.

[9] Sequestration is a mechanism that directs the President to cancel budget authority or other forms of budgetary resources in order to reach specified budget reduction targets. Balanced Budget and Emergency Deficit Control Act of 1985 (P.L. 99-177), often known as Gramm-Rudman-Hollings (GRH), introduced sequestration procedures into the federal budget process. Those sequestration procedures were modified in subsequent years to address separation of powers issues and other concerns. For details, see CRS Report R41901, *Statutory Budget Controls in Effect Between 1985 and 2002*, by Megan Suzanne Lynch.

[10] See CRS Report R41907, *A Balanced Budget Constitutional Amendment: Background and Congressional Options*, by James V. Saturno and Megan Suzanne Lynch.

[11] White House, Message from the President to the U.S. Congress, August 2, 2011, available at http://m.whitehouse.gov/the-press-office/2011/08/02/message-president-us-congress.

increase of $1.2 trillion.[12] That increase is also be subject to a joint resolution of disapproval. The President reportedly delayed that request to allow Congress to consider a disapproval measure.[13]

The third increase could also have been triggered in two other ways.[14] A debt limit increase of $1.5 trillion would have been permitted if the states had received a balanced budget amendment for ratification. A measure (H.J.Res. 2) to accomplish that, however, failed to reach the constitutionally mandated two-thirds threshold in the House in a 261–165 vote held on November 18, 2011.[15] The debt limit could also have been increased by between $1.2 trillion and $1.5 trillion had recommendations from the Joint Select Committee on Deficit Reduction, popularly known as the Super Committee, been reported to and passed by each chamber. If those recommendations had been estimated to achieve an amount between $1.2 trillion and $1.5 trillion, the debt limit increase would be matched to that figure. The Joint Select Committee, however, was unable to agree on a set of recommendations.

As neither of these two other options apply, the third increase in the debt limit would be $1.2 trillion, matching budget reductions slated to be made through sequestration and related mechanisms over the FY2013-FY2021 period.

The Debt Limit and the Treasury

Standard methods of financing federal activities or meeting government obligations used by the U.S. Department of Treasury (Treasury) can be hobbled when federal debt nears its legal limit. The government's income and outlays vary over the course of the year, producing monthly surpluses and deficits that affect the level of debt, whether or not the government has a surplus or deficit for the entire year. Even major government trust fund accounts that usually run annual surpluses can swing back and forth between deficits and surpluses on a month-to-month basis. The ability to borrow is central to Treasury cash management systems that handle fluctuations in federal revenues and outlays. When federal debt has neared the debt limit in the past, limiting the U.S. Treasury's borrowing authority, financial management has become more complicated.

If the U.S. Treasury were precluded from borrowing due to a binding debt limit in times when federal outlays outpaced revenues, the government would no longer meet all of its legal obligations in a timely manner.[16] If the limit prevents the Treasury from issuing new debt to manage short-term cash flows or to finance an annual deficit, the government may be unable to obtain the cash needed to pay its bills or it may be unable to invest the surpluses of designated government accounts (federal trust funds) in federal debt as generally required by law. In either case, the Treasury is left in a bind; the law requires that the government's legal obligations be paid, but the debt limit may prevent it from issuing the debt that would allow it to do so on time.

---

[12] For example, on December 30, 2011, debt subject to limit was $15,180 billion, just $14 billion below its statutory limit. The U.S. Treasury pays interest to Social Security and certain other trust funds in the form of Treasury securities at the end of June and December, which increases debt subject to limit.

[13] *CQ Roll Call Daily Briefing*, January 3, 2012.

[14] Congress may also consider a joint resolution of disapproval for this increase.

[15] Ratification requires approval by legislatures of three-fourths of the states. Article V specifies other means of amendment involving constitutional conventions as well.

[16] See CRS Report R41633, *Reaching the Debt Limit: Background and Potential Effects on Government Operations*, coordinated by Mindy R. Levit.

Among other consequences, a sustained inability to pay obligations on time could hinder the U.S. Treasury's ability to borrow on advantageous terms in the future. The Government Accountability Office has also concluded that delays in debt limit increases could lead to "serious negative consequences for the Treasury market and increase borrowing costs."[17] A delay in interest payments on Treasury securities would trigger a default and risk serious negative repercussions for economies and financial markets around the world. Default might be avoided in such situations by delaying other types of federal payments and transfers. A government that delays payment of an obligation, in effect, borrows from vendors, contractors, beneficiaries, state and local governments, or employees who are not paid on time. In some cases, delaying payments incurs interest penalties under some statutes such as the Prompt Payment Act, which directs the government to pay interest penalties to contractors if it does not pay them by the required payment date,[18] and the Internal Revenue Code, which requires the government to pay interest penalties if tax refunds are delayed beyond a certain date.[19]

Several credit ratings agencies and investment banks have expressed concerns about the consequences to the financial system and the economy if the U.S. Treasury were unable to fund federal obligations.[20] Many economists and financial institutions have stated that if the market associated Treasury securities with default risks, the effects on global capital markets could be significant.[21]

Past Treasury Secretaries, when faced with a nearly binding debt ceiling, have used special strategies to handle cash and debt management responsibilities. Actions taken in the past include suspending sales of nonmarketable debt, postponing or downsizing marketable debt auctions, and withholding receipts that would be transferred to certain government trust funds. Congress has authorized the Treasury Secretary to invoke a "debt issuance suspension period" to use some of these strategies using the Civil Service Retirement Fund and the Thrift Savings Fund, along with the authority to make those funds whole after an easing of the debt constraint.[22]

Some U.S. Treasury responses to the credit crunch that began in mid-2007 created balance sheet items that have expanded options available to the Treasury Secretary, although such options would have minor effects on delaying when federal debt would reach its legal limit. The U.S. Treasury began selling off certain mortgage-backed securities (MBSs) acquired in late 2008.[23]

---

[17] Government Accountability Office, *Debt Limit: Delays Create Debt Management Challenges and Increase Uncertainty in the Treasury Market*, GAO-11-203, February 22, 2011.

[18] 31 U.S.C. §3902.

[19] 26 U.S.C. §6611.

[20] Reuters, "S&P To Deeply Cut U.S. Ratings If Debt Payment Missed," June 29, 2011. For a summary of statements by the three major ratings agencies, see CRS Report R41932, *Treasury Securities and the U.S. Sovereign Credit Default Swap Market*, by D. Andrew Austin and Rena S. Miller.

[21] JP Morgan Chase, "The Domino Effect of a US Treasury Technical Default," U.S. Fixed Income Strategy Group Brief, April 19, 2011; Fitch Ratings, "Thinking the Unthinkable—What if the Debt Ceiling Was Not Increased and the US Defaulted?" June 8, 2011.

[22] For details, see out-of-print CRS Report 95-1109, *Authority to Tap Trust Funds and Establish Payment Priorities if the Debt Limit is not Increased*, by Thomas J. Nicola and Morton Rosenberg. Available upon request from the authors. 5 U.S.C. §8348(b) defines a debt issuance suspension period as "any period for which the Secretary of the Treasury determines for purposes of this subsection that the issuance of obligations of the United States may not be made without exceeding the public debt limit." After a debt issuance suspension period ends, the Treasury Secretary must report to Congress as soon as possible regarding fund balances and any extraordinary actions taken. For details, see 5 U.S.C. §8348(j,k).

[23] U.S. Treasury, "Treasury to Begin Orderly Wind Down of Its $142 Billion Mortgage-Backed Securities Portfolio," (continued...)

The pace of those sales was targeted at $10 billion per month in order to minimize any market disruptions in the mortgage securities market, and thus is unlikely to affect the timing of when the U.S. Treasury will reach the debt limit significantly. By the end of April 2011, the U.S. Treasury had sold $121 billion of its $225 billion portfolio of MBSs.[24] Even with proceeds of these or other potential asset sales however, the U.S. Treasury is unlikely to maintain smooth debt management operations indefinitely in the face of a continuing imbalance between federal revenues and outlays without an increase in the debt limit. U.S. Treasury contends that other types of asset sales are unlikely to provide a prudent or practical method of easing debt limit constraints.[25]

Why Have a Debt Limit?

The debt limit can hinder the Treasury's ability to manage the federal government's finances, as noted above. In extreme cases, when the federal debt is very near its statutory limit, the Treasury must take unusual and extraordinary measures to meet federal obligations.[26] While the debt limit has never caused the federal government to default on its obligations, it has at times caused great inconvenience and has added uncertainty to Treasury operations.

The debt limit also provides Congress with the strings to control the federal purse, allowing Congress to assert its constitutional prerogatives to control spending.[27] The debt limit also imposes a form of fiscal accountability that compels Congress and the President to take visible action to allow further federal borrowing when the federal government spends more than it collects in revenues. In the words of one author, the debt limit "expresses a national devotion to the idea of thrift and to economical management of the fiscal affairs of the government."[28] On the other hand, some budget experts have advocated elimination of the debt limit, arguing that other controls provided by the modern congressional budget process established in 1974 have superseded the debt limit, and that the limit does little to alter spending and revenue policies that determine the size of the federal deficit.[29]

(...continued)

press release, March 21, 2011, available at http://www.treasury.gov/press-center/press-releases/Pages/tg1111.aspx.

[24] Mary J. Miller, "MBS Wind Down Update—Taxpayers Have Now Recovered More than Half of Treasury's Original Investment," U.S. Treasury, *Treasury Notes*, May 2, 2011, available at http://www.treasury.gov/connect/blog/Pages/MBS-Wind-Down-Update-Taxpayers-Have-Now-Recovered-More-than-Half-of-Treasurys-Original-Investment.aspx.

[25] Mary Miller, Assistant Secretary of the Treasury for Financial Markets, "Federal Asset Sales Cannot Avoid Need for Increase in Debt Limit," Treasury Notes blog, May 6, 2011, available at http://www.treasury.gov/connect/blog/Pages/Federal-Asset-Sales-Cannot-Avoid-Need-for-Increase-in-Debt-Limit.aspx.

[26] U.S. General Accounting Office (GAO), *Analysis of Actions Taken during the 2003 Debt Issuance Suspension Period*, GAO-04-526, May 2004, available at http://www.gao.gov/new.items/d04526.pdf.

[27] For a vigorous assertion of the utility of the debt ceiling, see Anita S. Drishnakumar, "In Defense of the Debt Limit Statute," *Harvard Journal on Legislation*, vol. 42, 2005, pp. 135-185.

[28] Marshall A. Robinson, *The National Debt Ceiling: An Experiment in Fiscal Policy*, Washington, DC: The Brookings Institution, 1959, p. 5.

[29] Bruce Bartlett, "Why Congress Must Now Abolish its Debt Limit," *Financial Times*, October 22, 2009, p. 11; Brian C. Roseboro, Assistant Secretary for Financial Markets, U.S. Treasury, "Remarks to the Bond Market Association's Inflation-Linked Securities Conference", New York, NY, available at http://web.archive.org/web/20080709100455/http://www.treas.gov/press/releases/js506 htm.

A Brief History of the Federal Debt Limit

Origins of the Federal Debt Limit

Congress has always placed restrictions on federal debt. Limitations on federal debt have helped Congress assert its constitutional powers of the purse, of taxation, and the initiation of war. Between World War I and World War II the form of statutory restrictions on federal debt evolved into an aggregate limit that applied to nearly all federal debt outstanding.

Before World War I, Congress often authorized borrowing for specified purposes, such as the construction of the Panama Canal.[30] Congress also often specified which types of financial instruments Treasury could employ, and specified or limited interest rates, maturities, and details of when bonds could be redeemed. In other cases, especially in time of war, Congress provided the Treasury with discretion, subject to broad limits, to choose debt instruments.[31] Some opponents raised concerns that granting the Treasury Secretary authority to issue debt could affect monetary policies, which might tighten credit conditions. Proponents contended that federal borrowing would not disrupt settlements on such monetary issues reached in 1878 and 1890. Such concerns became moot after the establishment of the Federal Reserve System in 1913.

For example, the War Revenue Act of 1898 allowed Treasury to use certificates of indebtedness, which had maturities of a year or less, and were used for short-term borrowing and cash management, as well as long-term bonds.[32] For example, the 1898 War Revenue Act (30 Stat. 448-470) that funded Spanish-American War costs granted the Treasury Secretary the authority to have $100 million outstanding in certificates of indebtedness with maturities under a year, which were mainly sold to large investors, banks, and other financial institutions. The act also allowed the Treasury to issue $400 million in longer-term notes and bonds, which were made available to public subscription, allowing smaller investors to participate. Proponents of the act, however, made clear their intention to allow the Treasury Secretary substantial administrative leeway within those limits.[33]

Over time, the leeway granted the Treasury Secretary tended to expand. For example, the Second Liberty Bond Act of 1917, which helped finance the United States' entry into World War I, dropped certain limits on the maturity and redemption of bonds.[34] The act also incorporated unused borrowing capacity authorized by the First Liberty Bond Act (40 Stat 35; P.L. 65-3) and

---

[30] Spooner Act of June 28, 1902 (32 Stat 481; P.L. 57-183).

[31] Marshall A. Robinson, *The National Debt Ceiling: An Experiment in Fiscal Policy*, (Washington, DC: Brookings Institution, 1959), pp.1-6.

[32] The War Revenue Act was enacted June 13, 1898. Much of the legislative text of the act's public borrowing sections (§32, 33) were drawn from the acts of June 30, 1864, ch. 172, §1 (13 Stats. 218) and of March 3, 1865, ch. 77 (13 Stats. 469).

[33] See House debate, *Congressional Record*, vol. 31, part 6 (June 9, 1898), pp. 5713-5728; and Senate debate on June 10, 1898, pp. 5732-5749.

[34] P.L. 65-43, 40 Stat. 288, enacted September 24, 1917. See H. J. Cooke and M. Katzen, "The Public Debt Limit," *Journal of Finance*, vol. 9, no. 3 (September 1954), pp. 298-303. The Second Liberty Bond Act allowed purchases of government debt of allied (i.e., Entente) countries, which would have complicated limits on the final redemption of federal bonds issued to fund their purchase. Some federal bonds issued in the wake of the Panic of 1893 did not have maturity limits.

---

other previous borrowing acts.[35] Separate limits for previous debt issues, however, were retained in the text of that act—an overall aggregated debt limit evolved later. Features of debt authorized by previous acts, such as the broad tax exemption for First Liberty Bond Act securities, remained intact.

Subsequent borrowing measures were drafted as amendments to Second Liberty Bond Act until 1982.[36] Setting debt policy by amendments to the Second Liberty Bond Act of 1917 rather than through original statutes reflected changes in legislative drafting practices at that time.[37]

In the 1920s, Congress provided Treasury Secretary Andrew Mellon with additional leeway in order to replace expensive older federal debt with cheaper new issues. Congress allowed Treasury to issue notes, a financial instrument issued extensively in the Civil War and rarely thereafter, and limited the amount of notes outstanding, rather than the sum of issuances, which gave greater Treasury flexibility to roll over debt. Savings certificates designed for small investors were also reintroduced.[38]

In the 1930s, Congress moved towards aggregate constraints on federal borrowing that allowed the Treasury greater ability to respond to changing conditions and more flexibility in financial management. In March 1939, President Franklin Roosevelt and Treasury Secretary Henry Morgenthau asked Congress to eliminated separate limits on bonds and on other types of debt.[39] The House approved the measure (H.R. 5748) on March 23, 1939, the Senate passed it on June 1 (P.L. 76-201). When enacted on June 20, the measure created the first aggregate limit ($45 billion) covering nearly all public debt.[40] Combining a $30 billion limit on bonds with a $15 billion limit on shorter-term debt, while retaining the $45 billion total limit in effect, enabled Treasury to roll over maturing notes into longer-term bonds. This measure gave the Treasury freer rein to manage the federal debt as it saw fit. Thus, the Treasury could issue debt instruments with maturities that would reduce interest costs and minimize financial risks stemming from future interest rate changes.[41] While a separate $4 billion limit for "National Defense" series securities

---

[35] The other acts were the Panama Canal measure (Spooner Act; P.L. 57-183), the Payne-Aldrich Tariff Act of August 5, 1909 (36 Stat 11; P.L. 61-5); and two emergency bond measures passed in March 1917 (39 Stat 1002 and 39 Stat 1021).

[36] In 1982, the debt limit was codified into 31 U.S.C. §3101 by P.L. 97-258. Subsequent changes in the debt limit have been drafted as amendments to 31 U.S.C. §3101.

[37] Middleton Beaman, a former Law Librarian of the Library of Congress, Columbia Law School professor, and advocate for the professionalization of drafting legislation, returned to Washington in 1916 to assist the House Ways and Means Committee, which originated the Liberty Bond acts and other borrowing and revenue measures. This arrangement was formalized in 1918, when the Legislative Drafting Service, the predecessor office of the modern Office of Legislative Counsel, was established. Donald R. Kennon and Rebecca M. Rodgers, *The Committee on Ways and Means a Bicentennial History 1789-1989*, H. Doc. 100-244, p. 258. See also, Middleton Beaman, "Bill Drafting," *Law Library Journal*, vol. 7 (1914), pp. 64-71. For a critical view of legislative drafting in prior decades, see James Bryce, *The American Commonwealth*, 3rd revised ed., vol. 1 (New York: Macmillan, 1920), chapter XV on "Congressional Legislation."

[38] Revenue Act of November 23, 1921 (42 Stat 227; P.L.67-98). See also Paul Studenski and Herman E. Kroos, *Financial History of the United States*, 2nd ed. (New York: McGraw-Hill, 1963), p. 316.

[39] *New York Times*, "President Urges Ending of Limit on Bonded Debt; Asks Congress to Facilitate Borrowing by Eliminating $30,000,000,000, 'Ceiling' Stands By Total Debt Top $45 Billion All Right for Now, Message Says—Yielding to Economizers is Seen," March 21, 1939.

[40] P.L. 76-201. See also Senate debate, *Congressional Record*, vol. 84, part 6 (June 1, 1939), pp. 6480, 6497-6501.

[41] This limit did not apply to certain previous public debt issues that comprised a very minor portion of the federal debt.

was introduced in 1940, legislation in 1941 folded that borrowing authority back under an increased aggregate limit of $65 billion.[42]

Although the Treasury was delegated greater independence of action on the eve of the United States' entry into World War II, the debt limit at the time was much closer to total federal debt than it had been at the end of World War I. For example, the 1919 Victory Liberty Bond Act (P.L. 65-328) raised the maximum allowable federal debt to $43 billion, far above the $25.5 billion in total federal debt at the end of FY1919.[43] By contrast, the debt limit in 1939 was $45 billion, only about 10% above the $40.4 billion total federal debt of that time.[44]

World War II and After

The debt ceiling was raised to accommodate accumulating costs for World War II in each year from 1941 through 1945, when it was set at $300 billion.[45] After World War II ended, the debt limit was reduced to $275 billion. Because the Korean War was mostly financed by higher taxes rather than by increased debt, the limit remained at $275 billion until 1954. After 1954, the debt limit was reduced twice and increased seven times, until March 1962 when it again reached $300 billion, its level at the end of World War II. Since March 1962, Congress has enacted 76 separate measures that have altered the limit on federal debt.[46] Most of these changes in the debt limit were, measured in percentage terms, small in comparison to changes adopted in wartime or during the Great Depression. Some recent increases in the debt limit, however, were large in dollar terms. For instance, in May 2003, the debt limit increased by $984 billion and in February 2010 the debt limit was increased by $1.9 trillion (P.L. 111-139).

The Debt Ceiling in the Last Decade

During the four years (FY1998-FY2001) the government ran surpluses, federal debt held by intergovernmental accounts grew by $855 billion and debt held by the public fell by almost $450 billion. Since FY2001, however, debt held by the public has grown due to persistent and substantial budget deficits. Debt held in government accounts also has grown, in large part because Social Security payroll taxes have exceeded payments of beneficiaries. **Table 1** shows components of debt in current dollars and as percentages of gross domestic product (GDP).[47]

---

[42] Revenue Act of June 25, 1940 (54 Stat 516; P.L. 76-656) and Revenue Act of February 19, 1941 (55 Stat 7).

[43] U.S. Bureau of the Census, *Historical Statistics of the United States: Colonial Times to 1970*, H. Doc. 93-78 (Washington: GPO, 1975), Series Y 493-504.

[44] For a list of changes in the debt limit between September 1917 and 1941, see U.S. Treasury, *Statistical Appendix 1980*, Table 32 entitled "Debt limitation under the Second Liberty Bond Act, as amended, beginning 1917."

[45] Public Debt Acts of 1941 (P.L. 77-7), 1942 (P.L. 77-510), 1943 (78-34), 1944 (P.L. 78-333), and 1945 (P.L. 79-48).

[46] U.S. Office of Management and Budget, *FY2010 Budget of the U.S. Government: Historical Tables*, Table 7-3. Increases in the debt limited potentially enabled by the Budget Control Act of 2011 are counted as one alteration.

[47] Until 2001, Treasury publications did not divide debt subject to limit by that held by the public and that held by government accounts **Table 1** uses CRS calculations that approximate levels of debt subject to limit held in these two categories for fiscal years prior to 2001.

Figure 1 shows the components of federal debt as shares of gross domestic product (GDP) from FY1940 through FY2011, along with Administration projections through FY2016.[48] **Table 1** summarizes the increases in the debt limit from 1993-2011.[49]

---

[48] The data show components of debt compared to the size of the economy. This avoids possible distortions resulting from changing price levels over time and includes changes in per capita incomes. This percentage increases when debt grows faster than GDP and falls when it grows more slowly than GDP.

[49] For a list of debt limit votes, see CRS Report R41814, *Votes on Measures to Adjust the Statutory Debt Limit, 1978 to Present*, by Justin Murray. For a discussion of earlier debt limit increases, see out-of-print CRS Report 98-805 E, *Public Debt Limit Legislation: A Brief History and Controversies In the 1980s and 1990s*, by Philip D. Winters, which is available from the authors upon request.

Table 1. Components of Debt Subject to Limit, FY1996-FY2011

(in billions of current dollars and as percentage of GDP)

End of Fiscal Year	Debt Limit	Debt Subject to Limit					
		Total		Intragovernmental		Held by the Public	
		$ Billion	% of GDP	$ Billion	% of GDP	$ Billion	% of GDP
1996	5,500	5,137.2	66.6%	1,432.4	18.6%	3,704.8	48.0%
1997	5,950	5,327.6	64.9%	1,581.9	19.3%	3,745.8	45.6%
1998	5,950	5,439.4	62.8%	1,742.1	20.1%	3,697.4	42.7%
1999	5,950	5,567.7	60.5%	1,958.2	21.3%	3,609.5	39.2%
2000	5,950	5,591.6	56.9%	2,203.9	22.4%	3,387.7	34.5%
2001	5,950	5,732.8	56.1%	2,436.5	23.8%	3,296.3	32.2%
2002	6,400	6,161.4	58.4%	2,644.2	25.1%	3,517.2	33.4%
2003	7,384	6,737.6	61.4%	2,846.7	25.9%	3,890.8	35.4%
2004	7,384	7,333.4	62.8%	3,056.6	26.2%	4,276.8	36.6%
2005	8,184	7,871.0	63.2%	3,301.0	26.5%	4,570.1	36.7%
2006	8,965	8,420.3	63.7%	3,610.4	27.3%	4,809.8	36.4%
2007	9,815[a]	8,921.3	64.2%	3,903.7	28.1%	5,017.6	36.1%
2008	10,615[b]	9,960.0	69.2%	4,180.0	29.0%	5,780.3	40.2%
2009	12,104[c]	11,909.8	84.5%	4,358.0	30.9%	7,551.9	53.6%
2010	14,294[d]	13,510.8	93.1%	4,585.7	31.6%	9,022.8	62.2%
2011	15,194[e]	14,746.6	97.7%	4,663.3	30.9%	10,127.0	67.1%
Change during FY1998 - FY2001		$405.2		$854.6		$-449.5	
Change during FY2002 - FY2007		$3188.5		$1467.2		$1721.3	
Change during FY2008 - FY2011		$5825.3		$759.6		$5109.4	

Source: U.S. Department of the Treasury, Financial Management Service, *Treasury Bulletin*, June 2001 and December 2006. Bureau of the Public Debt, *Monthly Statement of Public Debt*, various issues. CRS calculations.

Notes: Amounts held by government accounts and held by the public for FY1996-FY2000 are approximated. In 2001, the Treasury publications began distinguishing holders of debt subject to limit. The numbers in the table showing this breakdown for FY1996 through FY2000 were calculated by subtracting debts of the Federal Financing Bank, an arm of the Treasury whose debt is subject to a separate limit, from intragovernmental debt. This calculation overestimates debt by billions of dollars because estimates of unamortized discount are unavailable. This adjusted amount was then subtracted from total debt subject to limit for an approximate measure of debt held by the public subject to limit. Because intragovernmental debt is overestimated, debt held by the public subject to limit is underestimated. Totals may not sum due to rounding.

a.   Debt limit increased September 29, 2007, to $9,815 billion.

b.   The debt limit was raised to $10,615 billion on July 30, 2008, and to $11,315 billion on October 3, 2008.

c.   Debt limit was increased February 17, 2009, to $12,104 billion.

d.   Debt limit was increased February 12, 2010, to $14,294 billion.

e.   Debt limit increased on August 2, 2011, to $14,694 billion and on September 22, 2011, to $15,194 billion.

Figure 1. Components of Federal Debt As a Percentage of GDP, FY1940-FY2016

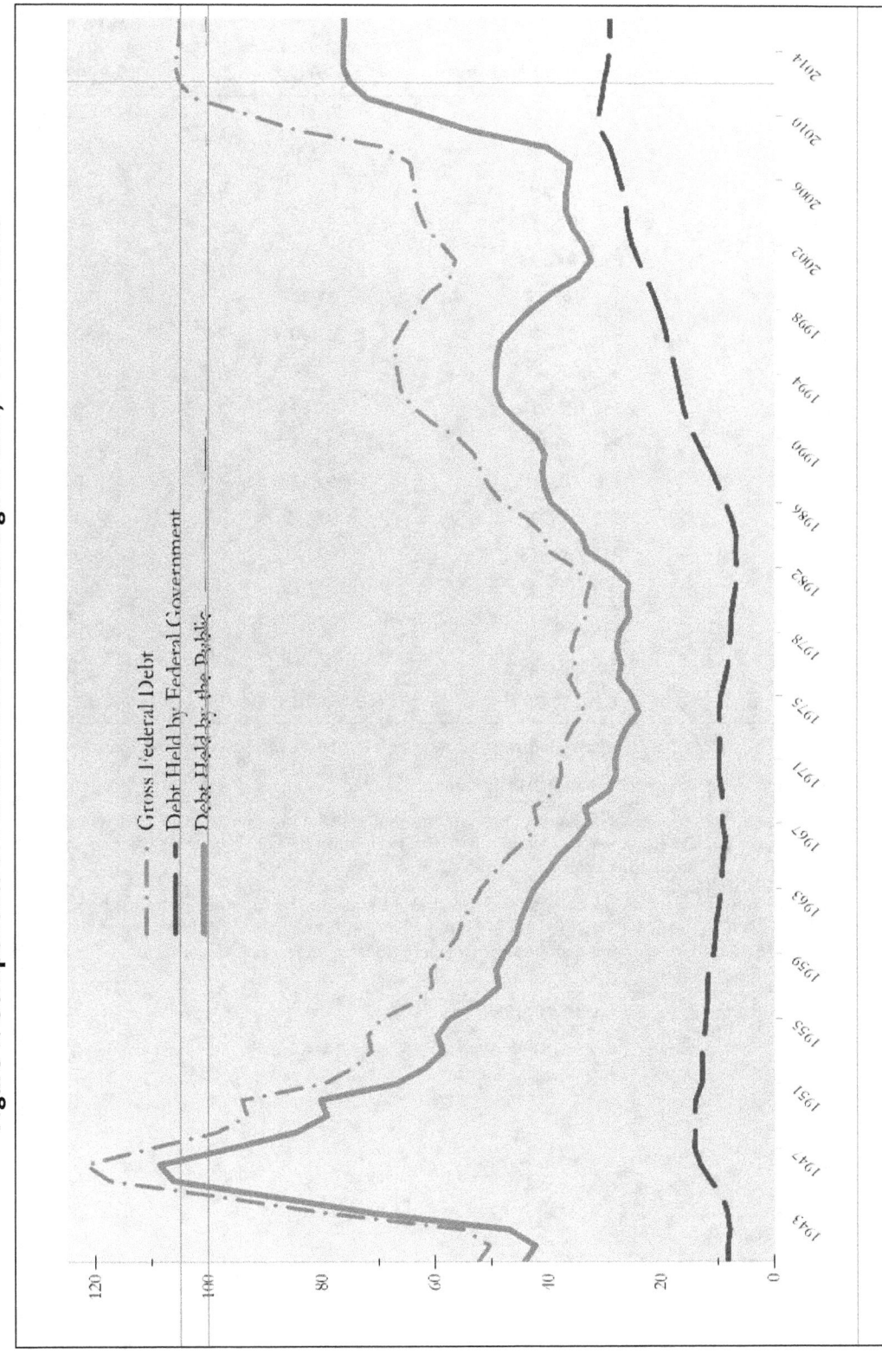

Source: CRS calculations based on FY2012 budget submission.

Notes: FY2011 values are estimated; FY2012-FY2016 values are OMB projections reflecting Administration assumptions and proposals.

Table 2. Increases in the Debt Limit 1993-2011

Date	Public Law (P.L.) Number	New Debt Limit ($ billion)	Change From Previous Limit ($ billion)
April 6, 1993	P.L. 103-12	$4,370[a]	$225
August 10, 1993	P.L. 103-66	4,900	530
February 8, 1996	P.L. 104-103	[b]	—
March 12, 1996	P.L. 104-115	[c]	—
March 29, 1996	P.L. 104-121	5,500	600[d]
August 5, 1997	P.L. 105-33	5,950	450
June 28, 2002	P.L. 107-199	6,400	450
May 27, 2003	P.L. 108-24	7,384	984
November 19, 2004	P.L. 108-415	8,184	800
March 20, 2006	P.L. 109-182	8,965	781
September 29, 2007	P.L. 110-91	9,815	850
July 30, 2008	P.L. 110-289	10,615	800
October 3, 2008	P.L. 110-343	11,315	700
February 17, 2009	P.L. 111-5	12,104	789
December 28, 2009	P.L. 111-123	12,394	290
February 12, 2010	P.L. 111-139	14,294	1,900
August 2, 2011	P.L. 112-25	15,194/16,394[e]	900/2,100[e]

Sources: CRS, compiled using the Legislative Information System, available at http://www.congress.gov; OMB.

a. Increased the debt limit temporarily through September 30, 1993.

b. Temporarily exempted from limit obligations in an amount equal to the monthly insurance benefits payable under Title II of the Social Security Act in March 1996, the exemption to expire on the earlier of an increase in the limit or March 15, 1996.

c. Temporarily exempted from limit (a) obligations in an amount equal to the monthly insurance benefits payable under Title II of the Social Security Act in March 1996 and (b) certain obligations issued to trust funds and other Federal Government accounts, both exemptions to expire on the earlier of an increase in the limit or March 30, 1996.

d. Difference from debt limit set on August 10, 1983.

e. See discussion in first section of this report. As of January 6, 2011, BCA-related increases totaled $900 billion, with a remaining option to increase the limit by $1,200 billion.

Federal debt held by government accounts has grown steadily since 1982, in part due to increases in Social Security taxes passed following recommendations of the 1983 Greenspan Commission, and reflecting the transition of the baby boom generation into its peak earnings years.[50]

Debt held by the public, which changes in response to total surpluses or deficits, grew as a share of GDP through the mid-1990s. After FY1992, deficits shrank, and from FY1998 through FY2001 the federal government ran surpluses.[51] Those surpluses, along with rapid GDP growth, reduced debt held by the public as a percentage of GDP. When large deficits returned and GDP growth slowed in the early 2000s, debt held by the public as a share of GDP again increased.

Smaller deficits in FY2006 and FY2007 led to smaller increases in publicly held debt. The total FY2007 deficit fell to 1.2% of GDP according to CBO, in part reflecting strong economic growth.[52] Financial turmoil in 2007 and 2008, however, and a subsequent recession that began in late 2007, led to federal actions taken to stabilize the housing and financial markets. The recession reduced federal revenues and increased federal spending, leading to large deficits and a series of debt limit increases. The future path of federal debt will depend on the pace of economic recovery as well as policy choices affecting federal spending and revenues.

The Debt Limit Issue in 2002

Accumulating debt in government accounts produced most of the pressure on the debt limit that occurred early in 2002. As deficits reemerged in FY2002, increases in debt held by the public added to the pressure on the debt limit in the spring of 2002. During the four fiscal years with surpluses (FY1998-FY2001), the increases in federally held debt and decreases in debt held by the public produced a net increase of $405 billion in total debt subject to limit. At the beginning of FY2002 (October 1, 2001), debt subject to limit was within $217 billion of the existing $5,950 billion debt limit.[53] Between then and the end of May 2002, debt subject to limit increased by another $217 billion, divided between a $117 billion increase in debt held by government accounts and a $100 billion increase in debt held by the public, putting the debt close to the $5,950 billion limit. **Table A-1**, presented in the **Appendix A**, shows month-by-month debt totals and accumulations from September 2001 through December 2010.

In the fall of 2001, the Administration recognized that a deteriorating budget outlook and continued growth in debt held by government accounts were likely to lead to the debt limit soon being reached. In early December 2001, it asked Congress to raise the debt limit by $750 billion to $6,700 billion. As the debt moved closer to and reached the debt limit over the first six months of FY2002, the Administration asked Congress repeatedly to increase the debt limit, warning of adverse financial consequences were the limit not raised.

---

[50] The Social Security Amendments of 1983 (H.R. 1900; P.L. 98-21), enacted April 20, 1983, introduced those changes. For details, see a summary available on the Social Security Administration's History website, at http://www.ssa.gov/history/1983amend2.html.

[51] Federal on-budget receipts and outlays nearly matched in FY1999, and the on-budget surplus in FY2000 was 0.9% of GDP. Prior to FY1999, the federal government last had an on-budget surplus in FY1960. Social Security receipts in excess of benefits make up most of the off-budget surplus, which has been positive since FY1985.

[52] U.S. Congress, Congressional Budget Office, An Analysis of the President's Budgetary Proposals for Fiscal Year 2009, March 2008, available at http://www.cbo.gov/ftpdocs/89xx/doc8990/03-19-AnalPresBudget.pdf.

[53] The debt limit was raised from $5,500 billion to $5,950 billion on August 5, 1997, as part of the Balanced Budget Act of 1997 (P.L. 105-33, 111 Stat. 251).

On April 4, 2002, the Treasury held debt below the limit by invoking its legislatively mandated authority to suspend reinvestment of government securities in the G-Fund of the federal employees' Thrift Savings Plan (TSP). This allowed the Treasury to issue new debt and meet the government's obligations. On April 15, debt subject to limit stood at $5,949,975 million, just $25 million below the limit. Once April 15 tax revenues flowed in, the Treasury "made whole" the G-Fund by restoring all of the debt that had not been issued to the TSP over this period and crediting the fund with interest it would have earned on that debt.[54] By the end of April, debt subject to limit had fallen back $35 billion below the limit.

Resolving the Debt Limit Issue in 2002

By the middle of May 2002, debt subject to limit had again risen to within $15 million of the statutory limit. At the FY2002 average spending rate, $15 million equaled about five minutes of federal outlays. The Treasury, for the second time in 2002, used its statutory authority to avoid a default. The Treasury's financing problems, however, would persist without an increase in the debt limit. On May 14, the Treasury asked Congress to raise the debt limit or enact other statutory changes allowing the Treasury to issue new debt. A Treasury news release stated "absent extraordinary actions, the government will exceed the statutory debt ceiling no later than May 16," and that

> a "debt issuance suspension period" will begin no later than May 16 [2002].... [This] allows the Treasury to suspend or redeem investments in two trust funds, which will provide flexibility to fund the operations of the government during this period.[55]

The Treasury reduced federal debt held by these government accounts by replacing it with non-interest-bearing, non-debt instruments, which enabled it to issue new debt to meet the government's obligations. The Treasury claimed these extraordinary actions would suffice, at the latest, through June 28, 2002. Without a debt limit increase by that date, the Treasury indicated it would need to take other actions to avoid breaching the ceiling. By June 21, the Treasury had postponed a regular securities auction, but took no other actions. With large payments and other obligations due at the end of June and at the beginning of July, the Treasury stated it would soon exhaust all options to issue debt and fulfill government obligations, putting the government on the verge of a default.

During May and June 2002, Congress took steps to increase the debt limit. The FY2002 supplemental appropriations bill (H.R. 4775) passed by the House on May 24 included, after extended debate, language allowing any eventual House-Senate conference on the legislation to increase the debt limit. However, the Senate's supplemental appropriations bill (S. 2551; incorporated as an amendment to H.R. 4775, June 3, 2002) omitted debt-limit-increasing language. The Senate leadership expressed strong reluctance to include a debt limit increase in the supplemental appropriation bill. Instead, on June 11, the Senate adopted a bill (S. 2578), without debate, to raise the debt limit by $450 billion to $6,400 billion. At that time, a $450 billion debt limit increase was thought to provide enough borrowing authority for government operations through the rest of calendar year 2002, if not through the summer of 2003. With the possibility of

---

[54] For a comprehensive discussion of the Treasury's previous uses of its short-term ability to avoid breaching the debt limit, see U.S. General Accounting Office, *Debt Ceiling: Analysis of Actions During the 1995-1996 Crisis*, GAO/AIMD-96-130, August 1996.

[55] U.S. Department of the Treasury, Treasury News, *Treasury Statement on the Debt Ceiling*, May 14, 2002.

default looming over it, the House passed the $450 billion debt limit increase by a single vote on June 27. The President signed the bill into law on June 28 (P.L. 107-199, 116 Stat. 734), ending the 2002 debt limit crisis.[56]

The Debt Limit Issue in 2003

On Christmas Eve, 2002, Kenneth Dam, Deputy Secretary of the Treasury, sent a letter to Congress requesting an unspecified increase in the debt limit by late February 2003, signaling that the $6,400 billion debt limit would then be reached.[57] The 108th Congress, still in the process of organizing itself, did not immediately respond. Through the winter and into the spring, the Treasury repeatedly requested that the debt limit be raised to avoid serious financial problems. By February 20, 2003, the Treasury, as in 2002, used legislatively mandated measures to manage debt holdings of certain government accounts to avoid reaching the debt limit. These actions included the replacement of internally held government debt with non-debt instruments in certain government accounts and not issuing new debt to these accounts. These actions allowed the Treasury to issue additional debt to the public to acquire the cash needed to pay for the government's commitments or to issue new debt to other federal accounts.

Through the rest of February and into May, the Treasury held debt subject to limit $15 million below the debt ceiling.[58] The adoption of the conference report on the FY2004 budget resolution (H.Con.Res. 95; H.Rept. 108-71) on April 11, 2003, in the House triggered the "Gephardt rule" (House Rule XXVII) that deems to have passed legislation (in this case, H.J.Res. 51) raising the debt limit to accommodate the spending and revenue levels approved in the adopted budget resolution.[59]

The Senate received the debt-limit legislation on April 11, but did not act until May 23, after receiving further Treasury warnings of imminent default. On that day, debt subject to limit was $25 million (or 0.0004%) below the existing $6,400 billion limit. The Senate adopted the legislation, after rejecting eight amendments and sent it to the President, who signed it on May 27. This legislation raised the debt limit to $7,384 billion (P.L. 108-24, 117 Stat. 710).

The Debt Limit Issue in 2004

In January 2004, CBO estimated that the debt limit, then set at $7,384 billion, would be reached the following summer.[60] In June 2004, the Treasury asked Congress to raise the debt limit in order

---

[56] For additional details, see U.S. General Accounting Office, *Debt Ceiling: Analysis of Actions During the 2002 Debt Issuance Suspension Period*, GAO-03-134, December 2002.

[57] Kenneth Dam, Deputy Secretary of the Treasury, letter to Speaker of the House, Dennis Hastert, December 24, 2002, available at http://www.treas.gov/press/releases/po3718.htm.

[58] The Treasury reduced the amount of debt held by selected federal accounts while it sold an equal (or smaller) amount of debt to the public. This raised cash needed to pay for ongoing obligations and kept the debt below the limit.

[59] The House Budget Committee has some discretion in setting the debt limit level in the House Joint resolution generated by the Gephardt rule. See CRS Report 98-453, *Debt-Limit Legislation in the Congressional Budget Process*, by Bill Heniff Jr. and CRS Report RL31913, *Developing Debt-Limit Legislation: The House's "Gephardt Rule"*, by Bill Heniff Jr.

[60] U.S. Congress, Congressional Budget Office, *The Budget and Economic Outlook: Fiscal Years 2005 to 2014*, January 2004.

to avoid the disruptions to government finances experienced in the previous two years.[61] In August, and again in September, the Treasury declared that the debt limit would be reached in the first half of October. On October 14, debt subject to limit reached $7,383,975 million, just $25 million below the existing limit. The Treasury employed methods used in the previous two years to keep debt under the legal limit. On October 14, Secretary of the Treasury John Snow informed Congress, just before the election recess, that available measures to avoid breaching the debt limit would be exhausted by mid-November.[62] Without an increase in the debt limit, the Treasury would be unable to meet all of the government's existing obligations, which could undermine the U.S. government's reputation in capital markets and raise costs of federal borrowing.

Although the House passed a budget resolution for FY2005 in the spring of 2004, it did not reach final agreement with the Senate on the measure. Without a budget resolution passed by Congress, no resolution to raise the debt limit could be deemed passed by the House automatically under the Gephardt rule. Consequently, no measure was available to send to the Senate. As the debt approached the limit through the summer and into the fall, no legislation was moved to raise the debt limit.

Earlier, in September 2004, the House had added an amendment to the FY2005 Transportation-Treasury appropriations (H.R. 5025) in an effort to remove the Treasury's flexibility in financing the government as federal debt approached and reached the existing limit. Without that flexibility, the government would be unable to meet its financial obligations as the amount of debt neared the limit. The legislation cleared the House, but the Senate did not act on it.

After the elections, Senator Frist, on November 16, 2004, introduced legislation (S. 2986) to raise the debt limit by $800 billion, from $7,384 billion to $8,184 billion. The Senate approved the increase on November 17, 2004. The House considered and approved the increase on November 18. The President signed the legislation into law (P.L. 108-415, 118 Stat. 2337) on November 19, 2004. Estimates made at that time anticipated the new limit would be reached between August and December 2005.

Shortly before the increase in the debt limit, the Treasury delayed a debt auction and informed Congress that it would invoke a "debt limit suspension period" as it had in previous years. The increase in the debt limit in mid-November allowed the Treasury to reschedule the debt auction and cancel, before it began, the "debt limit suspension period."

The Debt Limit Issue in 2005, 2006, and 2007

Debt limit increases in 2005, 2006, and 2007 took a less dramatic path than those in President Bush's first term. In 2005, Congress included three reconciliation instructions in the FY2006 budget resolution (H.Con.Res. 95, 109th Congress; April 28, 2005), the third of which directed the House Committee on Ways and Means and the Senate Finance Committee to report bills raising the debt limit. The instructions specified a $781 billion debt limit increase, to $8,965 billion, with a reporting date of no later than September 30, 2005. Neither committee reported a bill to raise the debt limit.

---

[61] Alan Fram, "Congress May Duck Debt Limit Raise," *Oakland Tribune*, June 5, 2004.

[62] John W. Snow, Secretary of the U.S. Treasury, letter to Senate Majority Leader Bill Frist, October 14, 2004, available at http://www.treas.gov/press/releases/reports/frist.pdf.

The adoption of the conference report on the FY2006 budget resolution in late April 2005 also triggered the Gephardt rule (House Rule XXVII), producing a House Joint Resolution (H.J.Res. 47) that also would raise the debt limit by $781 billion to $8,965 billion. Under the rule, the resolution was automatically deemed passed by the House and sent to the Senate. Through the end of the first session of the 109th Congress, the Senate had not considered H.J.Res. 47, nor had Congress considered a reconciliation bill raising the debt limit as called for in the budget resolution.

At the end of December 2005, Secretary of the Treasury Snow wrote Congress that the debt limit would probably be reached in mid-February 2006, although the Treasury could take actions that maintain the debt below its limit until mid-March. He therefore requested an increase in the debt limit.[63] In two more letters, sent on February 19 and March 6, Secretary Snow advised Congress that the Treasury was taking measures within its legal discretion to avoid reaching the limit and that these measures would suffice only until the middle of March 2006. Secretary Snow authorized actions used previously by the Treasury, including declaring a debt issuance suspension period. As March began, the government was again close to becoming unable to meet its obligations. During the week of March 13 the Senate took up H.J.Res. 47. On March 16, the Senate passed a debt limit increase after rejecting several amendments. The President's signature on March 20, 2006, then raised the debt limit (P.L. 109-182) to $8,965 billion.

In mid-May 2007, Congress passed the conference report (H.Rept. 110-153) on the FY2008 budget resolution. The House's Gephardt rule, triggered by the adoption of the conference report on the budget resolution, resulted in the automatic engrossment of a joint resolution (in this case, H.J.Res. 43, 110th Congress) raising the debt limit by $850 billion to $9,815 billion, and sending it to the Senate. At the end of July 2007, the Treasury asked Congress to raise the debt limit, stating the limit would be reached in early October 2007. In August, the CBO Director said that projections suggested that the limit would be reached in late October or early November. Without an increase, the Treasury indicated that it would take steps within its legal authority to avoid exceeding the debt limit. The Senate Finance Committee approved the House resolution (H.J.Res. 43) without changes on September 12, 2007. The Senate then passed the measure on September 27, which the President signed on September 29, 2007 (P.L. 110-91).

The Economic Slowdown and Federal Debt

Fiscal Policy Considerations

The U.S. economy is currently recovering slowly from a severe economic recession that began in December 2007 and ended in June 2009.[64] The economic slowdown began with a rapid deceleration of housing prices and a rise in interest rate spreads between private lending rates and benchmark Federal Reserve rates, indicating an increasing reluctance of major financial institutions to lend to each other as well as to firms and individuals. This led to sharply higher federal deficit spending in FY2008 spurred by several major actions taken by Congress to

---

[63] John W. Snow, Secretary of the Treasury, letter to Senator Max Baucus, December 29, 2005, available at http://www.ombwatch.org/files/budget/pdf/snow_debtlimit_2006.pdf.

[64] The end of a recession is said to occur when an economy has stopped shrinking, not when it has recovered. See National Bureau of Economic Research Business Cycle Dating Committee, press release, September 20, 2010, available at http://www.nber.org/cycles/sept2010 html.

unfreeze credit markets, boost consumption, and increase spending. Deficit spending was even higher in FY2009, with higher than average deficits as a percentage of GDP persisting into the next decade, likely leading to further increases in the federal debt and debt limit. While deficits for FY2010 were slightly lower and fiscal conditions are projected to improve in FY2011, deficits remain high relative to historical experience. Signs of economic weakness in mid-2011 have prompted concerns about the strength of the recovery and the possibility of a "double-dip" recession. President Obama proposed a package of measures aimed at increasing employment on September 8, 2011.

Economic recession affects the federal deficit in several ways. First, falling prices of many assets and equities can sharply reduce federal revenues from capital gains taxes and from the corporate tax. Second, individual income taxes, the largest component of federal revenues, may also fall if jobs are cut and unemployment increases due to economic conditions. Third, "automatic stabilizers" such as unemployment insurance and income support programs pay out more money as unemployment rises and the number of households eligible for means-tested benefits rises, thus increasing federal spending.

Boosting the economy through deficit spending provides a fiscal stimulus if the output levels of goods and services produced in the nation are below their potential levels. Deficit spending, however, can help accelerate inflation if output levels are near or at potential levels, and in addition, exacerbates long-term fiscal challenges. Several economists have expressed concerns that inflation, which had been relatively low since the early 1980s, could accelerate due to rising prices of food, energy, and primary commodities. While inflation would reduce the market value of the federal deficit, it would require Treasury to pay higher nominal interest rates on federal debt. The U.S. economy, however, is currently operating well below its potential, which has kept inflation at lower levels.

Raising the Debt Ceiling in 2008, 2009, and 2010

In a March 2008 report, CBO estimated the President's budget would lead to a $396 billion deficit in FY2008 and a $342 billion deficit in FY2009.[65] The actual deficit for FY2008 reached $455 billion. In August 2009, CBO estimated the deficit would total $1,587 billion in FY2009 and $1,381 billion in FY2010.[66] As a result of the current economic conditions and the actions of the federal government to bring the economy out of recession, the federal debt limit was raised twice in the second half of 2008 and twice in 2009.

The House Concurrent Resolution on the Budget (H.Con.Res. 312) recommended policies that would result in a $10,200 billion debt in FY2009. The Senate Concurrent Resolution on the Budget S.Con.Res. 70) recommended policies that would result in a total debt of $10,278 billion in FY2009.[67] Implementing either set of policies would require an increase in the federal debt

---

[65] U.S. Congress, Congressional Budget Office, *An Analysis of the President's Budgetary Proposals for Fiscal Year 2009*, Table 1.1, March 2008, available at http://www.cbo.gov/ftpdocs/89xx/doc8990/03-19-AnalPresBudget.pdf.

[65] U.S. Congress, Congressional Budget Office, *The Budget and Economic Outlook: An Update*, Table 1-1, August 2009, available at http://www.cbo.gov/doc.cfm?index=10521.

[66] Goldman Sachs U.S. Research, "US Daily: The Fiscal 2008 Deficit—Likely to Top $500 Billion," March 25, 2008.

[67] U.S. Congress, House Committee on the Budget, *Report to Accompany H. Con. Res. 312*, 110th Cong., 2nd sess., H.Rept. 110-543, March 2008, p. 99; U.S. Congress, Senate Committee on the Budget, *Report to Accompany S. Res. 70*, S.Prt. 110-039, March 2008.

limit. The conference agreement (H.Rept. 110-659) also recommended spending levels that would lead to a debt subject to limit of $10,207 billion in FY2009, a level that would require an increase in the statutory debt limit. The budget conference report passed the Senate on a 48-45 vote on June 4, 2008. The House passed the measure on the next day by a 214-210 vote. Agreement on the FY2009 budget resolution automatically created and deemed passed in the House legislation (H.J.Res. 92) that would increase the debt limit from its current level of $9,815 billion to $10,615 billion. Because the Senate did not take up H.J.Res. 92, the debt limit remained at $9,815 billion.

Subsequently, the House passed an amended version of the Housing and Economic Recovery Act of 2008 (H.R. 3221) by a vote of 272-152 that included a debt limit increase to $10,615 billion on July 23, 2008. The Senate then passed the measure on July 26 on a 72-13 vote. The President signed the bill on July 30 (P.L. 110-289), increasing the debt limit. In addition to increasing the debt limit, the act also contained provisions that would temporarily authorize the Secretary of Treasury to extend a line of credit to mortgage guarantee agencies Freddie Mac and Fannie Mae. The act also created the a new independent agency called the Federal Housing Finance Agency (FHFA), which replaced the Department of Housing and Urban Development Office of Federal Housing Enterprise Oversight (OFHEO) and the Federal Housing Finance Board (FHFB).

While CBO indicated that it was more likely than not that such intervention would not be needed, it also estimated a 5% chance of a cost to taxpayers of more than $100 billion.[68] Because debt subject to limit was just $339 billion less than the debt ceiling of $9,815 billion when the Senate passed H.R. 3221, some financial market participants may have worried that the debt limit, without an increase, might have hindered the Treasury Secretary's ability to intervene to support Freddie Mac and Fannie Mae. On September 7, 2008, the FHFA placed Fannie Mae and Freddie Mac in conservatorship, providing FHFA with the full powers to control the assets and operations of the firms.

Since the deprivatization of Fannie Mae and Freddie Mac, the federal government has acted to provide stability to financial markets.[69] On September 20, 2008, the U.S. Treasury submitted a proposal to Congress to authorize the Treasury Secretary to buy mortgage-related assets in order to stabilize financial markets. The Treasury proposal would allow Treasury holdings of mortgage-related securities up to $700 billion and would raise the debt limit to $11,315 billion.[70]

Representative Barney Frank proposed an amendment (Emergency Economic Stabilization Act of 2008) to a vehicle measure (H.R. 3997) that incorporated the main tenets of the Treasury proposal including raising the debt limit to $11,315 billion.[71] On September 29, 2008, however, the House rejected that amendment.

---

[68] U.S. Congress, Congressional Budget Office, *Cost Estimate for H.R. 3221 "Housing and Economic Recovery Act of 2008" As passed by the Senate on July 11, 2008, with an amendment transmitted to CBO on July 22, 2008*, July 24, 2008, available at http://www.cbo.gov/ftpdocs/95xx/doc9597/hr3221.pdf.

[69] For additional information see CRS Report RS22956, *The Cost of Government Financial Interventions, Past and Present*, by Baird Webel, Marc Labonte, and N. Eric Weiss.

[70] U.S. Department of Treasury, "Fact Sheet: Proposed Treasury Authority to Purchase Troubled Assets," Press release hp-1150, September 20, 2008, available at http://www.treas.gov/press/releases/hp1150 htm.

[71] U.S. Congress, House Financial Services Committee, Emergency Economic Stabilization Act of 2008 (Amendment to the Senate Amendment to H.R. 3997), available at http://www house.gov/apps/list/press/financialsvcs_dem/ amend_001_xml.pdf. For text of debt limit provision, see *Congressional Record*, (September 29, 2008), p. H10355.

On October 1, 2008, the Senate voted on, and passed, a different version of the Emergency Economic Stabilization Act of 2008 (H.R. 1424) that included the same debt limit increase.[72] The House passed H.R. 1424 on October 3, 2008, and it was signed into law by the President (P.L. 110-343) on the same day, raising the debt limit to $11,315 billion.

Current economic conditions led Congress to consider another economic stimulus measure. This measure contains both tax cuts and spending increases, which will increase the deficit by reducing revenues and increasing outlays. The American Recovery and Reinvestment Act of 2009 (ARRA) as passed by the Senate on February 10, 2009 (Division B of the Senate Substitute amendment to H.R. 1 and S. 350), contained a provision which would raise the debt limit to $12,140 billion. The version of this legislation originally passed by the House omitted this provision. The final conference agreement on ARRA was passed by the House and Senate on February 13, 2009, and signed by the President on February 17, 2009 (P.L. 111-5). This measure contained a provision increasing the debt limit to $12,104 billion.

The conference report on the Concurrent Resolution on the Budget for FY2010 (S.Con.Res. 13) recommended policies that would lead to a debt subject to limit of $13,233 billion in FY2010, a level that would require an increase in the statutory debt limit. The budget resolution also contained a revised estimate of debt subject to limit of $12,016 billion for FY2009. The adoption of this conference report on April 29, 2009, triggered the Gephardt rule (House Rule XXVII), producing a House Joint Resolution (H.J.Res. 45) that would raise the debt limit by $925 billion to $13,029 billion. Under the rule, the resolution was automatically deemed passed by the House and sent to the Senate.

In August 2009, according to media reports, Secretary of Treasury Timothy Geithner notified Congress that the debt limit would be reached in mid-October.[73] On November 4, the U.S. Treasury announced that it could postpone the time when federal debt would reach its statutory limit until the middle or the end of December.[74] Treasury dropped nearly $185 billion from its balance sheet by reducing the amount of loans available through the Supplemental Financing Program, an emergency loan program created in the days following Lehman Brothers' bankruptcy, from $200 billion to $15 billion, which extended the time until the debt limit would be reached.[75] According to media reports, the Obama Administration also contemplated scaling back the Troubled Asset Relief Program (TARP), which could also lower federal debt subject to statutory limit. Repayments of TARP funds by major financial institutions could also lower the amount of debt subject to limit.[76] Other measures, such as those taken in 2003 during a "debt issuance suspension period" (described above), could also have extended the U.S. Treasury's ability to operate within the debt limit. On the other hand, the U.S. Treasury was scheduled to issue $48 billion of nonmarketable securities to the FDIC on December 30 and to make interest

---

[72] U.S. Congress, Senate Banking, Housing, and Urban Affairs Committee, Emergency Economic Stabilization Act of 2008 (In the Nature of a Substitute to H.R. 1424), available at http://banking.senate.gov/public/_files/latestversionAYO08C32_xml.pdf.

[73] *CQ Weekly*, "Fall 2009 Outlook: Debt Limit Increase," September 7, 2009, p. 1966.

[74] U.S. Treasury, "November 2009 Quarterly Refunding Statement," press release tg346, November 4, 2009, http://www.ustreas.gov/press/releases/tg346 htm; David Clarke and CQ Staff, "Treasury Gives Congress More Breathing Room on Debt Limit," *CQ Today Online News*, November 4, 2009.

[75] For details, see Joseph Haubrich and John Lindner, "The Supplemental Financing Program," *Economic Trends*, Federal Reserve of Chicago, September 28, 2009, available at http://www.clevelandfed.org/research/trends/2009/1009/03monpol.cfm.

[76] *The Money Market Observer: Wrightson ICAP's Weekly Newsletter*, December 7, 2009.

---

payments to various federal trust funds on December 31 totaling about $100 billion, according to Wall Street analysts, which in the absence of a debt limit increase, could have challenged Treasury's debt management activities in the absence of special accounting measures.[77]

In mid-December, according to media reports, senior Members of the House chose to forgo a larger increase in the debt limit in favor of a smaller increase in the debt limit that would allow the U.S. Treasury Department to continue normal debt management operations for two months or so.[78] H.R. 4314, a measure to raise the debt limit to $12,394 billion, was introduced on December 15, 2009, and passed by the House the next day on a 218-214 vote. The Senate passed it on December 24 by a 60-39 vote, and the President signed the measure on December 28. On January 28, the Senate passed an amended version of H.J.Res. 45 on a 60-39 vote. The measure would raise the debt ceiling by $1,900 billion, to $14,294 billion.[79] In addition, one amendment to impose certain pay-as-you-go (PAYGO) restrictions was approved on a 60-40 vote.[80]

Some Members of Congress have called for the creation of a national commission to address federal debt and the government's fiscal situation, which could be enabled through a measure linked to an increase in the debt limit.[81] An amendment (S.Amdt. 3302 to S.Amdt. 3299) to H.J.Res. 45 that would have established a "Bipartisan Task Force for Responsible Fiscal Action" was not approved on a 53-46 vote, having failed to reach 60 votes, on January 26, 2010. President Obama then charged a National Commission on Fiscal Responsibility and Reform (Fiscal Commission) with identifying "policies to improve the fiscal situation in the medium term and to achieve fiscal sustainability over the long run."[82] The Fiscal Commission issued a report on December 1, 2010, and several commissioners issued their own fiscal proposals as well.[83]

The House approved H.J.Res. 45 on a 233-187 vote on February 4, forwarding the measure to the President. The Obama Administration had previously voiced its strong support for a debt limit increase.[84] The President signed the measure (P.L. 111-139) on February 12, 2010.

Raising the Debt Ceiling in 2011

On May 16, 2011, U.S. Treasury Secretary Timothy Geithner announced that the federal debt had reached its statutory limit and declared a debt issuance suspension period, which would allow

---

[77] *The Money Market Observer: Wrightson ICAP's Weekly Newsletter*, November 30, 2009.

[78] Paul Kane, "House Democrats Discard Larger Debt Limit," *Washington Post*, December 15, 2009, p. A4.

[79] *CQ Today Midday Update*, "Senate Sends Debt Ceiling Increase to House," January 28, 2010.

[80] S.Amdt. 3305. A second amendment (S.Amdt. 3300), approved on a 97-0 vote, provides certain protections to the Social Security program. Other amendments were not approved.

[81] Jonathan Weisman and John D. McKinnon, "White House Weighs New Panel to Tackle Deficit: Bipartisan Commission Considered As Administration Seeks to Show Resolve on a Problem that Dogs Its Broader Agenda," *Wall Street Journal*, November 26, 2009, p. A10.

[82] Executive Order 13531, "National Commission on Fiscal Responsibility and Reform," February 18, 2010; 75 FR 7927, February 23, 2010.

[83] National Commission on Fiscal Responsibility and Reform, *The Moment of Truth*, report, December 1, 2010, available at http://www.fiscalcommission.gov/sites/fiscalcommission.gov/files/documents/ TheMomentofTruth12_1_2010.pdf.

[84] U.S. Office of Management and Budget, "H.J.Res. 45—Increasing the Statutory Limit on the Public Debt," Statement Of Administration Policy, January 20, 2010, available at http://www.whitehouse.gov/omb/assets/sap_111/ saphjr45s_20100120.pdf.

---

certain extraordinary measures to extend Treasury's borrowing capacity until about August 2, 2011.[85] On July 1, 2011, the U.S. Treasury confirmed its view that its borrowing authority would be exhausted on that day.[86]

While many of the extraordinary measures have been used by previous Treasury Secretaries, the funding provided by those measures may buy much less time than in previous debt limit episodes. Given the size of the FY2011 federal deficit, projected to reach $1,399 billion according to the latest Congressional Budget Office (CBO) baseline estimates, those extraordinary measures may provide limited additional time before the federal government becomes unable to meet its financial obligations.[87]

Slowing the growth in federal debt by cutting spending had been suggested by some commentators as a means of avoiding an increase in the debt limit. The scale of required spending reductions, as of late spring 2011, would likely have approximately equaled total discretionary spending for the last five months of FY2011, which ended on September 30, 2011.[88]

On July 15, the U.S. Treasury announced that it had suspended reinvestment in the Exchange Stabilization Fund, one of the last available extraordinary measures before its borrowing authority (according to Treasury projections) would be exhausted on August 2.[89] One analyst, who had not expected this step to be taken until August 1, stated that the U.S. Treasury may have less headroom for cash management than previously anticipated.[90] Thus, funding federal operations could soon become increasingly complicated without a debt limit increase.[91] An independent analysis of Treasury cash flows, based on imputations from past Treasury reports, projects that from August 3 through the end of the month, cash inflows would total $174.4 billion, about $134.3 billion less than projected outflows of $306.7 billion.[92] Cash flow projections are subject to significant uncertainties.

Treasury estimates of when the debt limit would begin to bind and how long extraordinary measures would suffice to meet federal obligations have shifted since the Treasury Secretary's January 6, 2011, letter to Congress requesting a debt limit increase. Higher individual income tax revenues helped expand the headroom between the federal debt and its limit in late April. Sales of mortgage-backed securities (MBSs) also provided a relatively small amount of additional headroom. Estimates calculated by others of when Treasury would reach the debt limit and how

---

[85] Secretary of the U.S. Treasury Timothy Geithner, letter to Majority Leader Harry Reid, dated May 16, 2011, available at http://www.treasury.gov/connect/blog/Documents/20110516Letter%20to%20Congress.pdf.

[86] U.S. Treasury, "Treasury: No Change to August 2 Estimate Regarding Exhaustion of U.S. Borrowing Authority," Press release tg-1225, July 1, 2011, available at http://www.treasury.gov/press-center/press-releases/Pages/tg1225.aspx.

[87] U.S. Congressional Budget Office, "An Analysis of the President's Budgetary Proposals for Fiscal Year 2012," April 15, 2011, available at http://www.cbo.gov/doc.cfm?index=12130.

[88] For details, see CRS Report R41633, *Reaching the Debt Limit: Background and Potential Effects on Government Operations*, coordinated by Mindy R. Levit. The 2011 debt limit episode is described in the section entitled "Raising the Debt Ceiling in 2011."

[89] U.S. Treasury, "Update: As Previously Announced, Treasury to Employ Final Extraordinary Measure to Extend U.S. Borrowing Authority Until August 2," press release TG-1243, available at http://www.treasury.gov/press-center/press-releases/Pages/tg1243.aspx.

[90] Wrightson ICAP, *The Money Market Observer*, July 18, 2011.

[91] Wrightson ICAP, *The Money Market Observer*, May 2, 2011.

[92] Bipartisan Policy Center, "Debt Limit Analysis," June 27, 2011, available at http://www.bipartisanpolicy.org/sites/default/files/Debt%20Ceiling%20Analysis%20FINAL_0.pdf.

---

long extraordinary measures would extend federal borrowing capacity have typically been close to Treasury's estimates.[93] Such estimates require analysis of federal spending patterns, the pace of federal debt redemptions and refinancings, and the inflow of receipts, each of which is subject to uncertainties.

The Treasury Secretary, in a letter to Congress dated May 2, 2011, had indicated that he would declare a debt issuance suspension period on May 16, unless Congress acted beforehand, which would allow certain extraordinary measures to extend Treasury's borrowing capacity until early August 2011.[94] Certain measures that rely on the Treasury Secretary's existing authority, such as the draw-down of the Supplementary Financing Program (SFP), have already taken place. The SFP, an initiative intended to help manage monetary policy, had been drawn down from $200 billion to $5 billion to provide additional headroom under the limit.[95] New issues of State and Local Government Series (SLGS) Treasury securities were suspended on May 6, 2011.

On January 6, 2011, Treasury Secretary Geithner sent a letter to Senate Majority Leader Harry Reid requesting an increase in the debt limit. At that time, Secretary Geithner stated that federal debt would likely reach its statutory limit between March 31 and May 16, 2011.[96] On April 4, the Treasury Secretary wrote Congress that estimates indicated that federal debt would reach its limit between April 15 and May 31, 2011.[97] The U.S. Treasury had also previously projected that its borrowing capacity, even using extraordinary measures, would be exhausted about July 8, 2011.[98]

A bill (H.R. 1954) to raise the debt limit to $16,700 billion was introduced on May 24 and was defeated in a May 31, 2011, House vote of 97 to 318. The House passed the Cut, Cap, and Balance Act of 2011 (H.R. 2560; 234-190 vote) on July 19, 2011. On July 22, the Senate tabled the bill on a 51-46 vote. The measure would have increased the statutory limit on federal debt from $14,294 billion to $16,700 billion once a proposal for a constitutional amendment requiring a balanced federal budget was transmitted to the states.

On July 25, 2011, legislation entitled the Budget Control Act of 2011 was introduced in different forms by both House Speaker Boehner (House Substitute Amendment to S. 627) and Majority Leader Reid (S.Amdt. 581 to S. 1323). Subsequently, on August 2, 2011, President Obama signed into law a revised compromise measure (Budget Control Act; BCA; P.L. 112-25), following House approval by a vote of 269-161 on August 1, 2011, and Senate approval by a vote of 74-26 on August 2, 2011. This measure included numerous provisions aimed at deficit reduction and an

---

[93] Wrightson ICAP, *The Money Market Observer*, May 2, 2011; Secretary of the U.S. Treasury Timothy Geithner, letter to Majority Leader Harry Reid, dated January 6, 2011, available at http://www.treasury.gov/connect/blog/Documents/Letter.pdf.

[94] Secretary of the U.S. Treasury Timothy Geithner, letter to Speaker John Boehner, dated May 2, 2011, available at http://www.treasury.gov/connect/blog/Documents/FINAL%20Debt%20Limit%20Letter%2005-02-2011%20Boehner.pdf. The same text was sent to all Members.

[95] U.S. Treasury, "Treasury Announces Marketable Borrowing Estimates," press release TG-1155, May 2, 2011, available at http://www.treasury.gov/press-center/press-releases/Pages/tg1155.aspx.

[96] Paul M. Krawzak, "Showdown Ahead on Debt Limit as Geithner Urges Action," *CQ Today Online News*, January 6, 2011; Secretary of the U.S. Treasury Timothy Geithner, letter to Majority Leader Harry Reid, dated January 6, 2011.

[97] U.S. Treasury, "Treasury Issues Updated Debt Limit Projections," March 1, 2011, available at http://www.treasury.gov/press-center/press-releases/Pages/tg1084.aspx.

[98] Secretary of the U.S. Treasury Timothy Geithner, letter to Majority Leader Harry Reid, dated April 4, 2011, available at http://www.treasury.gov/connect/blog/Documents/FINAL%20Letter%2004-04-2011%20Reid%20Debt%20Limit.pdf.

increase in the debt limit of up to $2.4 trillion that would occur in several stages (see section on BCA for details). These provisions would eliminate the need for further increases in the debt limit until late 2012 or early 2013.

The Coming Trajectory of Federal Debt and Deficits

The size of the debt may remain a concern in the future due to the size of impending federal deficits necessitating further increases in the debt limit. CBO warns that the current trajectory of federal borrowing is unsustainable and could lead to slower economic growth in the long run as debt rises as a percentage of GDP. The total federal deficit rose trebled from $455 billion in FY2008 to $1,413 billion in FY2009, fell slightly to $1,294 billion in FY2010, and nudged higher to $1,2999 billion in FY2011.[99] Much of the increase in deficits can be attributed to weak economic and financial market turmoil that started in late 2007, as well as to federal responses.

Nonetheless, many budget experts remain concerned that a slow economic recovery or a "double-dip" recession could keep federal revenues below previous trendline projections for several years, and that the federal government would continue to run large deficits.

---

[99] U.S. Congressional Budget Office, *The Budget and Economic Outlook: An Update*, August 19, 2010, p. 1, available at http://www.cbo.gov/doc.cfm?index=11705; *Joint Statement of Timothy Geithner, Secretary of the Treasury, and Jacob Lew, Director of the Office of Management And Budget, on Budget Results for Fiscal Year 2011*, U.S. Treasury press release TG-1328, October 14, 2011, available at http://www.treasury.gov/press-center/press-releases/Pages/tg1328.aspx.

Concluding Comments

Since the late 1950s, the federal government increased its borrowing from the public in all years, except in FY1969 following imposition of a war surcharge and in the period FY1997-FY2001. The persistence of federal budget deficits has required the government to issue more and more debt to the public.[100] The accumulation of Social Security and other trust funds, particularly after 1983 when recommendations of the Greenspan Commission were implemented, led to sustained growth in government-held debt subject to limit.[101] The growth in federal debt held by the public and in intergovernmental accounts, such as trust funds, has periodically obliged Congress to raise the debt limit.

Between August 1997, when the debt limit was raised to $5,950 billion, and the beginning of FY2002 in October 2001, federal budget surpluses reduced debt held by the public. In early 2001, the 10-year budget forecasts projected large and growing surpluses, indicating rapid reduction in debt held by the public. Some experts expressed concern about consequences of retiring all federal debt held by the public.[102] Most long-term forecasts computed at that time, however, showed large deficits emerging once the baby boomers began to retire. Short-term forecasts projected continuous growth in debt held by government accounts, largely due to the difference between Social Security tax revenues and benefit payments. The combination of falling levels of publicly held debt and rising levels of debt held by government accounts moderated the expected growth of total debt. The moderate growth in total debt those projections had forecast was expected to postpone the need to increase the debt limit until late into the decade, when accumulating debt in government accounts would overtake reductions in debt held by the public. Once budget projections were released in 2002, however, expectations of large, persistent surpluses were smashed and hopes for reductions in debt held by the public collapsed.

The financial crisis of 2007-2009 and the subsequent economic recession led to large federal deficits that accelerated the growth of total debt, which necessitated a series of debt limit increases. Past experience suggests that direct fiscal costs of a financial crisis, such as costs of bailing out financial institutions, is dwarfed by the effects of diminished tax revenues and elevated social safety net benefits.[103] Debate during the 2011 debt limit episode reflected a growing concern with the fiscal sustainability. Over the next decade, without major changes in federal policies, persistent and possibly growing deficits, along with the ongoing growth in the debt holdings of government accounts, would increase substantially the amount of federal debt subject to limit. Unless federal policies change, Congress would repeatedly face demands to raise the debt limit to accommodate the growing federal debt in order to provide the government with the means to meet its financial obligations.

---

[100] The ability to run fiscal deficits gives the federal government useful flexibility in managing its finances, although large deficits may harm economic performance. See CRS Report RL33657, *Running Deficits: Positives and Pitfalls*, by D. Andrew Austin.

[101] *Report of the National Commission on Social Security Reform*, January 1983, available at http://www.ssa.gov/history/reports/gspan.html.

[102] Testimony of Federal Reserve Chairman Alan Greenspan, in U.S. Congress, Senate Committee on the Budget, *Outlook for the Federal Budget and Implications for Fiscal Policy*, hearings, 107th Cong., 1st sess., January 25, 2001, available at http://www.federalreserve.gov/boarddocs/testimony/2001/20010125/default.htm.

[103] Carmen M. Reinhardt and Kenneth S. Rogoff, *This Time is Different: Eight Centuries of Financial Folly*, (Princeton: Princeton, NJ, 2009).

Further Reading

Drishnakumar, Anita S., "In Defense of the Debt Limit Statute," *Harvard Journal on Legislation*, vol. 42, 2005, pp. 135-185.

Kenneth D. Garbade, *Birth of a Market: The U.S. Treasury Securities Market from the Great War to the Great Depression*, Cambridge: MIT Press, 2012.

Gordon, John Steele, *Hamilton's Blessing: the Extraordinary Life and Times of Our National Debt*, New York: Penguin, 1998.

Hormats, Robert D., *The Price of Liberty: Paying for America's Wars from the Revolution to the War on Terror*, New York: Times Books, 2007.

Noll, Franklin, "The United States Public Debt, 1861 to 1975," EH.Net Encyclopedia, edited by Robert Whaples, May 26, 2004. Available at http://eh.net/encyclopedia/article/noll.publicdebt.

Carmen M. Reinhardt and Kenneth S. Rogoff, *This Time is Different: Eight Centuries of Financial Folly*, Princeton, 2009.

Wright, Robert E., *One Nation Under Debt: Hamilton, Jefferson, and the History of What We Owe*, New York: McGraw-Hill, 2008.

Appendix A. Debt Subject to Limit by Month Since September 2001

Table A-1 provides data on the dollar amount, in current dollars, of federal debt and the changes in these amounts by month between the end of September 2001 (the end of FY2001) and the end of December 2010. The table shows outstanding monthly balances, subject to the debt limit, of total federal debt, debt held by government accounts, and debt held by the public.

All three measures of debt subject to limit increased over this period. From the end of September 2001 (the end of FY2001) to the end of September 2011, total federal debt increased by $9,014 billion, debt held in government accounts increased by $2,203 billion, and debt held by the public increased by $6,811 billion. All three measures experienced periodic reductions in some months. Because federal receipts and outlays are spread unevenly over the fiscal year, debt may rise or fall in a given month, even if debt measures follow an overall increasing trend.

Table A-1. Debt Subject to Limit by Month, September 2001-December 2011

(in millions of current dollars)

End of Month	Total	Change from Previous Period	Held by Government Accounts	Change from Previous Period	Held by the Public	Change from Previous Period
Sept. 2001	$5,732,802	—	$2,436,521	—	$3,296,281	—
Oct. 2001	5,744,523	$11,721	2,451,815	$15,294	3,292,709	$-3,572
Nov. 2001	5,816,823	72,300	2,469,647	17,832	3,347,176	54,467
Dec. 2001	5,871,413	54,590	2,516,012	46,365	3,355,401	8,225
Jan. 2002	5,865,892	-5,521	2,525,755	9,743	3,340,138	-15,263
Feb. 2002	5,933,154	67,262	2,528,494	2,739	3,404,659	64,521
Mar. 2002	5,935,108	1,954	2,528,318	-176	3,406,789	2,130
Apr. 2002	5,914,816	-20,292	2,549,438	21,120	3,365,378	-41,411
May 2002	5,949,975	35,159	2,553,350	3,912	3,396,625	31,247
June 2002	6,058,313	108,338	2,630,646	77,296	3,427,667	31,042
July 2002	6,092,050	33,737	2,627,980	-2,666	3,464,070	36,403
Aug. 2002	6,142,835	50,785	2,620,946	-7,034	3,521,890	57,820
Sept. 2002	6,161,431	18,596	2,644,244	23,298	3,517,187	-4,703
Oct. 2002	6,231,284	69,853	2,680,812	36,568	3,550,472	33,285
Nov. 2002	6,294,480	63,196	2,680,788	-24	3,613,692	63,220
Dec. 2002	6,359,412	64,932	2,745,787	64,999	3,613,625	-67
Jan. 2003	6,355,812	-3,600	2,753,301	7,514	3,602,511	-11,114
Feb. 2003	6,399,975	44,163	2,750,471	-2,830	3,649,504	46,993
Mar. 2003	6,399,975	0	2,722,812	-27,659	3,677,163	27,659
Apr. 2003	6,399,975	0	2,731,042	8,230	3,668,933	-8,230

End of Month	Total	Change from Previous Period	Held by Government Accounts	Change from Previous Period	Held by the Public	Change from Previous Period
May 2003	6,498,658	98,683	2,755,895	24,853	3,742,763	73,830
June 2003	6,625,519	126,861	2,842,361	86,466	3,783,158	40,395
July 2003	6,704,814	79,295	2,835,566	-6,795	3,869,247	86,089
Aug. 2003	6,743,775	38,961	2,829,387	-6,179	3,914,388	45,141
Sept. 2003	6,737,553	-6,222	2,846,730	17,343	3,890,823	-23,565
Oct. 2003	6,826,668	89,115	2,869,493	22,763	3,957,175	66,352
Nov. 2003	6,879,626	52,958	2,879,117	9,624	4,000,509	43,334
Dec. 2003	6,952,893	73,267	2,940,736	61,619	4,012,157	11,648
Jan. 2004	6,966,851	13,958	2,951,219	10,483	4,015,633	3,476
Feb. 2004	7,049,163	82,312	2,953,123	1,904	4,096,040	80,407
Mar. 2004	7,088,648	39,485	2,941,195	-11,928	4,147,453	51,413
Apr. 2004	7,089,700	1,052	2,960,151	18,956	4,129,549	-17,904
May 2004	7,151,523	61,823	2,973,869	13,718	4,177,653	48,104
June 2004	7,229,320	77,797	3,039,987	66,118	4,189,334	11,681
July 2004	7,271,328	42,008	3,033,396	-6,591	4,237,933	48,599
Aug. 2004	7,305,531	34,203	3,037,149	3,753	4,268,382	30,449
Sept. 2004	7,333,350	27,819	3,056,590	19,441	4,276,760	8,378
Oct. 2004	7,383,975	50,625	3,096,207	39,617	4,287,768	11,008
Nov. 2004	7,464,740	80,765	3,087,834	-8,373	4,376,906	89,138
Dec. 2004	7,535,644	70,904	3,158,531	70,697	4,377,114	208
Jan. 2005	7,567,702	32,058	3,171,089	12,558	4,396,615	19,501
Feb. 2005	7,652,726	85,024	3,176,406	5,317	4,476,320	79,705
Mar. 2005	7,715,503	62,777	3,175,460	-946	4,540,042	63,722
Apr. 2005	7,704,041	-11,462	3,185,364	9,904	4,518,677	-21,365
May 2005	7,717,574	13,533	3,207,232	21,868	4,510,342	-8,335
June 2005	7,778,128	60,554	3,280,914	73,682	4,497,214	-13,128
July 2005	7,829,029	50,901	3,278,725	-2,189	4,550,304	53,090
Aug. 2005	7,868,395	39,366	3,284,696	5,971	4,583,699	33,395
Sept. 2005	7,871,040	2,645	3,300,969	16,273	4,570,071	-13,628
Oct. 2005	7,964,782	93,742	3,345,589	44,620	4,619,193	49,122
Nov. 2005	8,028,918	64,136	3,351,093	5,504	4,677,826	58,633
Dec. 2005	8,107,019	78,101	3,424,304	73,211	4,682,715	4,889
Jan. 2006	8,132,290	25,271	3,442,543	18,239	4,689,747	7,032
Feb. 2006	8,183,975	51,685	3,457,409	14,866	4,726,567	36,820
Mar. 2006	8,281,451	97,476	3,443,602	-13,807	4,837,849	111,282

End of Month	Total	Change from Previous Period	Held by Government Accounts	Change from Previous Period	Held by the Public	Change from Previous Period
Apr. 2006	8,262,718	-18,733	3,479,623	36,021	4,783,095	-54,754
May 2006	8,263,812	1,094	3,492,648	13,025	4,771,165	-11,930
June 2006	8,330,646	66,834	3,566,186	73,538	4,764,460	-6,705
July 2006	8,352,614	21,968	3,569,550	3,364	4,783,064	18,604
Aug. 2006	8,423,321	70,707	3,576,166	6,616	4,847,155	64,091
Sept. 2006	8,420,278	-3,043	3,622,378	46,212	4,828,972	-18,183
Oct. 2006	8,498,016	77,738	3,650,241	27,863	4,847,775	18,803
Nov. 2006	8,545,715	47,699	3,649,736	-505	4,895,979	48,204
Dec. 2006	8,592,513	46,798	3,724,450	74,714	4,868,063	-27,916
Jan. 2007	8,619,499	26,986	3,737,894	13,444	4,881,605	13,542
Feb. 2007	8,690,921	71,422	3,744,299	6,405	4,946,622	65,017
Mar. 2007	8,760,735	69,814	3,740,127	-4,172	5,020,608	73,986
Apr. 2007	8,753,070	-7,665	3,778,255	38,128	4,974,815	-45,793
May 2007	8,740,892	-12,178	3,792,201	13,946	4,948,691	-26,124
June 2007	8,779,168	38,276	3,867,819	75,618	4,911,348	-37,343
July 2007	8,845,417	66,249	3,873,239	5,420	4,972,178	60,830
Aug. 2007	8,918,493	73,076	3,854,115	-19,124	5,064,377	92,199
Sept. 2007	8,921,343	2,850	3,903,710	49,595	5,017,633	-46,744
Oct. 2007	8,994,639	73,296	3,958,357	54,647	5,036,281	18,648
Nov. 2007	9,065,827	71,188	3,950,468	-7,889	5,115,358	79,077
Dec. 2007	9,144,715	78,888	4,038,566	88,098	5,106,149	-9,209
Jan. 2008	9,155,842	11,127	4,053,199	14,633	5,102,644	-3,505
Feb. 2008	9,275,683	119,841	4,045,007	-8,192	5,230,676	128,032
Mar. 2008	9,358,135	82,452	4,051,685	6,678	5,306,450	75,774
Apr. 2008	9,298,567	-59,568	4,080,887	29,202	5,217,680	-88,770
May 2008	9,324,137	25,570	4,071,992	-8,895	5,252,144	34,464
June 2008	9,427,901	167,869	4,169,509	134,950	5,258,392	32,920
July 2008	9,520,220	92,319	4,144,377	-25,132	5,375,843	117,451
Aug. 2008	9,580,508	60,288	4,129,413	-14,964	5,451,095	75,252
Sept. 2008	9,959,850	379,342	4,179,574	50,161	5,780,276	329,181
Oct. 2008	10,504,702	544,852	4,231,878	52,304	6,272,824	492,548
Nov. 2008	10,595,725	91,023	4,228,270	-3,608	6,367,454	94,630
Dec. 2008	10,640,274	44,549	4,298,482	70,212	6,341,792	-25,662
Jan. 2009	10,569,310	-70,964	4,278,424	-20,058	6,290,886	-50,906
Feb. 2009	10,814,630	245,320	4,261,734	-16,690	6,552,896	262,010

End of Month	Total	Change from Previous Period	Held by Government Accounts	Change from Previous Period	Held by the Public	Change from Previous Period
Mar. 2009	11,066,217	251,587	4,258,272	-3,462	6,807,946	255,050
Apr. 2009	11,178,827	112,610	4,273,005	14,733	6,905,822	97,876
May 2009	11,260,445	81,618	4,265,719	-7,286	6,994,725	88,903
June 2009	11,487,470	227,025	4,336,673	70,954	7,150,797	156,072
July 2009	11,611,178	123,708	4,299,673	-37,000	7,311,505	160,708
Aug. 2009	11,755,205	144,027	4,294,923	-4,750	7,460,282	148,777
Sept. 2009	11,853,434	98,229	4,325,124	30,201	7,528,311	68,029
Oct. 2009	11,836,629	-16,805	4,372,308	47,184	7,464,321	-63,990
Nov. 2009	12,057,363	220,734	4,367,935	-4,373	7,689,428	225,107
Dec. 2009	12,254,506	197,143	4,466,279	98,344	7,788,227	98,799
Jan. 2010	12,222,507	-31,999	4,485,502	19,223	7,737,005	-51,222
Feb. 2010	12,383,717	161,210	4,469,373	-16,129	7,914,344	177,339
Mar. 2010	12,716,511	332,794	4,448,645	-20,728	8,267,866	353,522
Apr. 2010	12,892,729	176,218	4,480,458	31,813	8,412,271	144,405
May 2010	12,992,539	99,810	4,498,120	17,662	8,494,419	82,148
June 2010	13,149,560	157,021	4,537,716	39,596	8,611,844	117,425
July 2010	13,185,208	35,648	4,504,601	-33,115	8,680,607	68,763
Aug. 2010	13,398,794	213,586	4,493,418	-11,183	8,905,376	224,769
Sept. 2010	13,510,840	112,046	4,509,632	16,214	9,001,208	95,832
Oct. 2010	13,617,337	106,497	4,568,895	59,263	9,048,442	47,234
Nov. 2010	13,809,121	191,784	4,555,396	-13,499	9,253,725	205,283
Dec. 2010	13,972,513	163,392	4,603,888	48,492	9,368,625	114,900
Jan. 2011	14,078,501	105,985	4,614,179	10,291	9,464,322	95,697
Feb. 2011	14,142,331	63,830	4,597,775	-16,403	9,544,556	80,233
Mar. 2011	14,217,862	75,531	4,587,082	-10,693	9,630,780	86,225
Apr. 2011	14,235,938	18,076	4,601,684	14,602	9,634,253	3,472
May 2011	14,293,975	58,038	4,591,014	-10,671	9,702,961	68,708
June 2011	14,293,975	0	4,572,152	-18,862	9,721,823	18,862
July 2011	14,293,975	0	4,558,417	-13,735	9,735,558	13,735
Aug. 2011	14,638,920	344,946	4,634,731	76,314	10,004,189	268,631
Sept. 2011	14,746,553	107,633	4,639,427	4,697	10,107,126	102,937
Oct. 2011	14,948,905	202,352	4,712,667	73,239	10,236,237	129,112
Nov. 2011	15,110,499	161,593	4,720,541	7,874	10,389,958	153,720
Dec. 2011	15,180,337	69,838	4,775,277	54,736	10,447,663	57,705

Sources: U.S. Treasury, Bureau of the Public Debt, *Monthly Statement of the Public Debt*, Sept. 2001-Nov. 2011, available at http://www.treasurydirect.gov/govt/reports/pd/mspd/mspd.htm; CRS calculations. Dec. 2011 data computed from Daily Treasury Statement.

Appendix B. Major Debt Measures Before the Entry of United States into World War II

Table B-1. Major Federal Debt Measures, 1898-1941

Statutes at Large	Title	Bill	Public Law
30 Stat. 448	War Revenue Act of June 13, 1898	H.R. 10100	n.a.
32 Stat. 481	Spooner Act of June 28, 1902	—	n.a.
36 Stat. 11	Payne-Aldrich Tariff Act of August 5, 1909	H.R. 1438	P.L. 61-5
40 Stat. 35	First Liberty Bond Act of April 24, 1917	H.R. 2762	P.L. 65-3
40 Stat. 288	Second Liberty Bond Act of September 24, 1917	H.R. 5901	P.L. 65-43
40 Stat. 502	Third Liberty Bond Act of April 4, 1918	H.R. 1123	P.L. 65-120
40 Stat. 844	Fourth Liberty Bond Act of July 9, 1918	H.R. 12580	P.L. 65-192
40 Stat. 1309	Victory Liberty Loan Act of March 3, 1919	H.R. 16136	P.L. 65-328
42 Stat. 227	Revenue Act of November 23, 1921	H.R. 8245	P.L. 67-98
46 Stat. 19	Act of June 17, 1929	H.R. 1648	P.L. 71-11
46 Stat. 775	Act of June 17, 1930	H.R. 1244	P.L. 71-376
46 Stat. 1506	Act of March 3, 1931	H.R. 16111	P.L. 71-820
48 Stat. 337	Gold Reserve Act of January 30, 1934	H.R. 6976	P.L. 73-87
49 Stat. 20	Act of February 4, 1935	H.R. 4304	P.L. 74-3
52 Stat. 447	Act of May 26, 1938	H.R. 10535	P.L. 75-552
53 Stat. 1071	Act of July 20, 1939	H.R. 5748	P.L. 76-201
54 Stat. 516	Revenue Act of June 25, 1940	H.R. 10039	P.L. 76-656
55 Stat. 7	Revenue Act of February 19, 1941	H.R. 2959	P.L. 77-7

Source: *Statutes at Large*, various volumes, Kenneth D. Garbade, *Birth of a Market: The U.S. Treasury Securities Market from the Great War to the Great Depression* (Cambridge: MIT Press), forthcoming 2012.

Notes: Public law (P.L.) enumeration before the 1930s was not as consistently or commonly used as at present. Table 7.3 of the FY2012 Budget *Historical Tables* volume lists measures since 1940 (available at http://www.whitehouse.gov/sites/default/files/omb/budget/fy2012/assets/hist07z3.xls).

n.a. = not available.

Author Contact Information

D. Andrew Austin
Analyst in Economic Policy
aaustin@crs.loc.gov, 7-6552

Mindy R. Levit
Analyst in Public Finance
mlevit@crs.loc.gov, 7-7792